Bugs, Bugs, Bugs!

Dragonflies

by Margaret Hall

Consulting Editor: Gail Saunders-Smith, PhD

Consultant: Laura Jesse, Extension Associate
Department of Entomology
Iowa State University
Ames, Iowa

Capstone
press
Mankato, Minnesota

Pebble Plus is published by Capstone Press,
151 Good Counsel Drive, P.O. Box 669, Mankato, Minnesota 56002.
www.capstonepress.com

1 2 3 4 5 6 10 09 08 07 06 05

Library of Congress Cataloging-in-Publication Data
Hall, Margaret, 1947–
  Dragonflies / by Margaret Hall.
  p. cm.—(Pebble Plus. Bugs, bugs, bugs!)
  Includes bibliographical references and index.
  ISBN-13: 978-0-7368-4252-5 (hardcover)
  ISBN-10: 0-7368-4252-7 (hardcover)
  ISBN-13: 978-0-7368-6125-0 (softcover pbk.)
  ISBN-10: 0-7368-6125-4 (softcover pbk.)
  1. Dragonflies—Juvenile literature. I. Title. II. Series.
QL520.H35 2006
595.7'33—dc22   2004029486

Summary: Simple text and photographs describe the physical characteristics of dragonflies.

Editorial Credits
Heather Adamson, editor; Linda Clavel, set designer; Ted Williams, book designer; Jo Miller, photo researcher;
  Scott Thoms, photo editor

Photo Credits
Corel, back cover
Dwight R. Kuhn, 17
Gerald D. Tang, 5
KAC Productions/Larry Ditto, front cover
Minden Pictures/Foto Natura/Cisca Castelijns, 6–7; Rene Krekels, 18–19
Nature Picture Library, 21
Pete Carmichael, 13
Peter Arnold, Inc./Ed Reschke, 1, 10–11
Photri MicroStock/J. Taylor, 14–15
Visuals Unlimited/John and Barbara Gerlach, 9

Note to Parents and Teachers

The Bugs, Bugs, Bugs! set supports national science standards related to the diversity of
life and heredity. This book describes and illustrates dragonflies. The images support
early readers in understanding the text. The repetition of words and phrases helps early
readers learn new words. This book also introduces early readers to subject-specific
vocabulary words, which are defined in the Glossary section. Early readers may need
assistance to read some words and to use the Table of Contents, Glossary, Read More,
Internet Sites, and Index sections of the book.

Table of Contents

What Are Dragonflies? 4

How Dragonflies Look 6

What Dragonflies Do 14

Glossary 22

Read More 23

Internet Sites 23

Index 24

What Are Dragonflies?

Dragonflies are long, colorful insects with large wings.

How Dragonflies Look

Dragonflies have four wings.
Their wings are
thin and clear.
Some wings have
colored marks.

Some dragonflies are
as long as a child's finger.
Other dragonflies are
as long as a child's hand.

Dragonflies have
two big eyes.
They can see a small bug
across a yard.

eyes

Dragonflies have
strong mouths.
They crunch
and chew bugs.

mouth

What Dragonflies Do

Dragonflies fly quickly.
Some dragonflies can go
almost as fast as a car.

Dragonflies hold their legs
in the shape of a net.
They swoop through the air
and catch insects
with their legs.

Dragonflies can mate
while they fly.
Male dragonflies hold the
females when they mate.

Female dragonflies
lay eggs on water.
Young dragonflies
hatch from the eggs.

Glossary

female—an animal that can give birth to young animals or lay eggs

hatch—to break out of an egg

insect—a small animal with a hard outer shell, six legs, three body sections, and two antennas; most insects have wings.

male—an animal that can father young

mate—to come together to make young

Read More

Jacobs, Liza. *Dragonflies.* Wild, Wild, World. San Diego: Blackbirch Press, 2003.

Morris, Ting. *Dragonfly.* Creepy Crawly World. North Mankato, Minn.: Smart Apple Media, 2005.

St. Pierre, Stephanie. *Dragonfly.* Bug Books. Chicago: Heinemann Library, 2002.

Internet Sites

FactHound offers a safe, fun way to find Internet sites related to this book. All of the sites on FactHound have been researched by our staff.

Here's how:

1. Visit *www.facthound.com*

2. Type in this special code **0736842527** for age-appropriate sites. Or enter a search word related to this book for a more general search.

3. Click on the **Fetch It** button.

FactHound will fetch the best sites for you!

Index

eggs, 20

eyes, 10

fly, 14, 18

food, 12, 16

hunting, 16

legs, 16

mate, 18

mouths, 12

size, 4, 8

speed, 14

wings, 4, 6

young, 20

Word Count: 124
Grade: 1
Early-Intervention Level: 14